# A Song Will Arise

A collection of uplifting, themed,
reflective poems

Barbara Todd

Freedom Publishing
12 Dukes Court, Bognor Road,
Chichester, PO19 8FX, United Kingdom
www.freedompublishing.net

ISBN: 978-1-908154-63-7

British Library Cataloguing in Publication Data. A catalogue record for this book is available from the British Library

Formatted by Freedom Publishing
Cover by Esther Kotecha, EKDesign
Printed in the United Kingdom

# Contents

**Songs to the Father**

# Endorsements

The Old Testament poet was inspired to write with enthusiasm that there was "rejoicing" over God's creation and a "delighting" in the human race at the beginning of time. And just as singing was present in a previous millennium, there will also be a "new song" in the world to come (Proverbs 8; Revelation 5).

So, Barbara's theme in respect of the singing that is taking place between these two epochs is a necessary reminder of its value and of the importance of the words being conveyed through the music. The tone of those songs she brings in the first half of this compilation may be in a lower key, but even so there can be discerned a glimpse of hope and anticipation woven within them. The second half sees the tempo being raised, capturing in the songs that emerge a fuller realisation of what it means to know God as our Shepherd and Father.

The rich and wide-ranging vocabulary that Barbara shares with us within each one of these songs enhances the harmonies being played and brings lush colour to the pictures in our minds. The vibrancy and melodies contained within these poems indeed help bring the realisation to readers that there is a song in all of us.

**Steve Bishop**
*A Premier Praise radio broadcaster, 'The Way' website contributor, speaker at retreats and conferences and author of numerous books including 'Dialogue with a Donkey' and 'Two Minutes Added on', Steve now publishes under his own Bible-Bish-Books label.*

I have found that these poems, or songs, very much resonate with my own observations and reflections through these recent years of challenge, but they also bring to bear new observations and reflections that reveal more of the hope that leads us from darkness to light. The poet has a unique voice, but like all good poets Barbara has the skilful ability to make universal what is personal to her. I heartedly recommend this book to you – and may it be, like it has been for me - a rich resource for getting in touch with the 'song that is in all of us'.

**Sarah Fordham**

*Sarah Fordham is on the secretariat of Integral, a global alliance of Christian relief and development agencies, as their Marketing and Communications Co-ordinator. She is a church leader in north London and is herself an author and poet whose published works include 'Psalm Readings', 'Love's First Touch' and 'In the Cool of the Day', and she is the convenor of the Abide Poetry Club.*

As you read, or even have the privilege of this eclectic group of poems being read to you, know that you are in the presence of a wordsmith. Barbara's creative ability and skill is thoughtful and inspirational, and her poems can be challenging to the perceptive reader. Her reflections on life are written with heavenly creativity, and are gloriously descriptive, expanding the imagination with meaningful pictures. Barbara's words bring an honest message of hope in a paradoxical world.

**Rev Steve Hepden**

*Rev Steve Hepden is an ordained minister of the Elim Church. He has years of experience in church leadership, church planting, conference speaking, counselling and pastoral and prophetic ministry both in the UK and abroad. His most recent books 'Rejection Hurts' and 'The Orphan Heart' have also been published by Freedom Publishing.*

# Acknowledgements

I am grateful to all those of my family and friends who have encouraged me in my poetry writing journey, and to those who have given me opportunities to share my poems in meetings, events and concerts, or have used them in their own gatherings.

My special thanks go to the wonderful members of The Abide Poetry Club, who, together with our convener Sarah Larkin, have been a continuous source of stimulation and inspiration, and to my dear friend Will Watson, who has both supported and encouraged me along the way, and has once again kindly acted as my proof-reader and text editor. Thanks also go to David Powell from Freedom Publishing and to my friend, and now prolific author and publisher, Stephen Bishop of Bible-Bish-Books.

# Introduction

Like so many during the unprecedented circumstances of the past couple of years, I turned to a number of creative activities in order to try to keep myself occupied and upbeat during the tedious long-covid induced lockdowns. In April 2020, therefore, when invited to join a poetry writers' group which had for some time been run by a friend in north London, I jumped at the chance. I had no notion at that point that over two years later, I would still be enjoying its weekly zooms and that a third published volume of my poetry would ensue. Sarah Larkin's once monthly Abide Poetry Club started meeting weekly on zoom at the start of the initial lockdown, and became a fountain of life, joy, support and creativity for all those who participated in it. Most of the poems in this book have been shared with, and critiqued by, that poetry group.

**A Song Will Arise** comprises four themed collections of poems which together encourage us to reflect on and consider our own lives and situations, and to turn away from those things which would do damage to ourselves and to our world. You will, as with my previous volumes, notice a number of allusions to songs and singing, for poems are, after all, songs without music. The title of this volume, 'A Song Will Arise', comes from the poem 'Freedom' in 'Songs for the Journey'.

The collections are:

**Songs from the Earth:** this is a group of poems about our world, including some which describe the magnificent variety of our weather, the seasons and the natural environment, and others which lament the wanton disregard and destruction of our planet by its human inhabitants. The sequence of Ripples poems considers the so-called 'butterfly effect' of how even minuscule changes, both positive and negative, can result in hugely different significant outcomes.

**Songs of the children**: these are poems about the human condition and the difficulties and issues people so often face, and indeed themselves cause, including several poems on both the theme of mirrors and that of war. This collection heads eventually in a positive direction, ending with poems about love, peace and blessing.

**Songs for the shepherd**: this group of poems is based around the themes contained in the well-known Psalm 23, 'The Lord is My Shepherd'. These poems are reflective and spiritual in nature and would be helpful to use in times of prayer and meditation, both individually and corporately. They encourage us to draw aside from the hectic pace of our lives and to be still.

**Songs to the Father**: these poems are based around the Lord's Prayer and its big themes of Heaven, God's will, sin, evil and glory. These too would serve well as meditations and prayers, in both personal and church or school settings. They encourage us to look inwards at ourselves and outwards and upwards, at God and at His everlasting kingdom.

The poem '**Spitfire**' was written for the 80th anniversary of The Battle of Britain, and is dedicated to my son in law Mike Collett of Ultimate Aerobatics, who flies and works with WW2 Warbirds.

The poem '**There's a song in all of us**' was written for, and is dedicated to, the lovely Mitcham Community Choir, of which I am a member.

# Songs from the Earth

A collection of poems
about our world

# Winter

The light is thin now
And the icy air brittle, easily cracked
Like the frozen strands
Suspended from the doorframe
Over a miraculous overnight appearing
Of white spidery tracery crawling across the
panes
This is dragon weather
Moist hot breath hanging mid-air on the winter
chill
Blowing its fire into shivery mittened hands
A warming glow that all too quickly fades
Sudden biting gusts unkindly lash legs
While booted feet crunch across steely grey
grass
Avoiding ice-stricken puddles
And proudly ridged frozen furrows
Could it be too cold to snow
But high above, the heavy whitened sky
Looks pregnant with the anticipated
precipitation
And soon it will indeed burst open
Delivering its precious burden to the world
below
Each tiny gift gracefully gliding down
Whilst exuberant children and dogs
Dance excitedly in the whiteness
Trying to catch one on their tongue

# Snowfall

An unexpected, mysterious hush
Has descended upon us
For the night worked its magic
Leaving an unbroken crystalline carpet
Glinting and twinkling startling-white
Under the pale winter morning sun
Draw back the curtains and gasp
At this oh so infrequent delight
This sudden transformation of the world
Crisp small mounds run atop every wall
Every window ledge, every washing line
The usual brownness, greenness gone
Buried beneath this nocturnal outpouring
Subnivean bushes desperately
Poke their frozen limbs upwards through the
whiteness
Hoping to thaw out in the sun's meagre heat
Forlorn trees longing for the thaw
Desperately huddle together for warmth
Though none is forthcoming
And shake their branches
To rid themselves of their chilly cloaks
Closer inspection of this icy miracle
Reveals dozens of tiny twig-like footprints
Minute breaks in the pristine smoothness
Encircling the bird feeders
Small feet scurrying to locate
Any hope of sustenance
And we too long to rush outside
To make our mark
On this unsullied terrain
That has been unfurled before us

# Spring

Seam between Winter and Summer
Herald of light and warmth
How we have fantasised about your advent
Through these dark, dreary winter-tide days
Renewer of hope of brightness
Master of winds and tides
Haltingly you edge us forward
Towards those so hankered-after, languid
summertime days
A scattering of yellow and purple
Flung across green
Whilst above
Pink fragile blossoms
At the mercy of your buffeting
Alert us to your abrupt arrival
Your watery predilection
Casts an eruption of greenness
Along every once-bare bough
Long our minds have conjured up
This unfurling of freshness
This scent of newness
The awakening of life long dormant
Deep beneath its brooding blanket
But now aroused from repose
Seamlessly drifting
Towards a salutation of Summer
Meanwhile, you delight us
With your gentle palette
Of life's first flush

# These hot days

There is no hiding place
On these sweltering hot days
Nowhere to run
From the oppressive beating down of the sun
No shade that provides sufficient escape
From its implacable gaze
And no shadow that can cast
A cooling spell
Over these sultry times
This stifling heat
Brings with it a languid listlessness
That is difficult to shake off
For its scorching torridity
Drains out all energy
Every desire for action
Every hope of movement
For all but the mad dogs
Who run about in the midday sun
The parched ground
Reveals shimmering mirages
Enticing false hopes of refreshment
When in reality
There is only an endless aridity
And these hot days
Just stretch relentlessly onward
With no evident end in sight

# Sky red

Sun red, heavens red, shepherds' delight
Promise red, sinking towards the night
Shimmering red, cloud red, day unfurled
Wispy red, all the sky cotton curled
Roasting red, burning red, fading fast
Red hot, cooling down, dark at last
Day's end, eventide, light gone
Nightfall, all must rest, day's done

Red returning, red emerging, sailors' warning
Outset red, indicating stormy morning
Cool red, gentle red, glory rising
Dawn red, all of night soon hiding
Red ascending, start of day's gentle hue
Racing red, interrupting sky's blue
Day spring, nature stirring, night shun
Sunrise, all awakened, day's begun

# Storm brewing

These clouds are brooding
With malicious intent
With their dark, oppressive, almost tangible
heaviness
They are determined
To strike fear into every heart
Their strident anger bringing an unnatural
stillness
That is not the stillness of peace
But the stillness
Of a latent feeling of impending doom
Here no leaf trembles
No bird sings
And wayward cats have long since returned
home
All are waiting now for that distant sound
That rolling releaser of tension
Of the pressure holding us all bound
These past hours
Ears straining on heads
That have been weighed down, uneasy
Are hoping, longing
For that first rumble
That first solitary drop
The harbingers
Of their liberation

# Walking through storms

Its wuthering wildness is terrifying
This tempestuous, boisterous wind
Buffets me along
Its strong gusts propelling me
In directions I did not intend to go
How can I even remain upright
When these furious squalls
Seem to have a mind of their own
A desire to sweep me off my feet
And drive me hither and thither
This howling gale
Sends wild creatures
Scurrying back to their boltholes
And boats to lower their anchors
In the nearest harbour
Is it wise to walk
Through such a storm
When overhead branches
Are viciously ripped off unsuspecting trees
And anxious saplings are unkindly uprooted
From their earthy fixings
Should I too
Rapidly retreat to a safe haven
And await the return of
A more peaceful day

# Such rain

Such rain
Furiously hammering down on rooves
Aggressively bombarding windowpanes
As if trying to force entrance
Into our private spaces
Such a frenzied precipitation
Its fearsome needle-like shards
Violently attacking hapless pedestrians
Provoking their shrieking and howling
As they fearfully scurry
To hide for safety in doorways
And under the hoped-for umbrella-like canopy
Of any nearby tree
Deep, unfamiliar pools form at street corners
And down through grills
We can hear the torrents
Deep in the bowels of the city
Turbulently rushing and swirling
Will there be floods?
Yet still we are grateful for
This angry monsoon-like deluge
For after so much barren dryness
As all living things wilted
Parched for lack of rain
This much-needed relief
From prolonged thirst
Is welcome

# Floods

The heavens disgorged
An unexpected deluge
Causing a cascade of unfriendly torrents
Tumbling down hillsides
Pouring off buildings
Racing along streets
An unstoppable force
A violent, vicious assault
No respecter of persons or property this
Or even of nature itself
Everything under attack
No stone left unturned
An inconceivable power
A force that could not be reckoned with
Hills brought low
Huge craters formed without warning
Green fields ploughed into unnecessary furrows
Homes floating downstream to unknown
destinations
A surreal scene
Everything gone
Devastated, swept away
Life overthrown in an instant
A mud-coloured filter
Of spewed-up soil, silt and sewage
Enveloping all
An apocalyptic scene
All sense of happiness and well-being
Snatched away
By this unwanted invader

# Moon

How high the moon
Rides across the ink-jet sky
Seemingly motionless
The path of its nocturnal journey
Eluding us
Evading us
Such imperceptible motion
Appearing stationary, immobile
As shimmering silver-white, it rests there

How high the moon
Gleams through the celestial night
Such ethereal beauty
Calling to us
Captivating us
Held fast in wonder
We stand and gaze into the vast heavens
Unable to fully fathom
Its many mysteries

How high the moon
Floats in its starry home
With so few travellers
Voyaging there
Visiting its alien lands
It is still such an enigma
So awestruck, moonstruck
We nightly look out, look up
Pondering this miraculous appearing

# Tumbleweed

Spinning and rolling
Across barren wastelands
And desolate desert places
Propelled by scorching winds
The tumbleweed is picked up
And tossed helplessly about
Frail, feeble and flimsy
Its shallow roots can no longer hold it secure
In the hard, parched earth
With no stable structure
It is torn from the ground
By the wind's vigorous gusts
And with no purpose in mind
It is blown hither and thither
Always out of control
Vulnerable, rootless, aimless
Directionless but driven about
Totally at the mercy of the wind
Like a lost soul it roams
Through the empty spaces
Of a land where nothing much grows
As it rolls endlessly onwards
The tumbleweed scatters its seeds randomly
Hoping that at least something, somewhere
Will eventually result from its erratic
wanderings

# Trees

So tall they stand
These majestic guardians of our world
Their lives
Breathe life into us all
So high they rise
Gracefully, in imperceptible increments
Out from the dark, damp earth
Until stately, they tower above us all
Such freshness in the variegated greenness
Of their fronds and needles
So firm and sturdy these pillars
In each, the wisdom of years
What do they know or understand
Of our world
Our battles and petty squabbles
Our ruinous tendencies
Our evident descent toward destruction
Do they sigh
Do they despair
Over us
Are they angry
At our wanton annihilation
As holding up the sky with their arms
They transfer their life's breath
Into ours

# The rape of the earth

Does the Earth remember
That pristine time
When in the cool of the day
All was new and fresh
And everything was beautiful
Does the ground cry out in anger
When it is choked with the constant fumes
From a never-ending stream
Of greedy, guzzling monsters charging through
What is not truly theirs
Uprooting and displacing
Everything in their wake
Does the Earth howl in anguish
When its green and pleasant lands
Are burned and bulldozed
Ripped up and raped by those who would
Destroy their wild, lush magnificence
Robbing it of its treasures
For their own gain
Are its once crystal clear waters
Now riven with the flotsam and jetsam
Of lives succumbed to disposability
And the polluting effluence
Of manifold excesses
Dreaming of more peaceful times
When no alien thing sullied their azure blueness
Or disturbed the myriad of their creatures
Is the Earth groaning, remembering a different
day
Is it straining on tiptoe
To catch a glimpse of the time when
All wrongs will finally be righted
And it will, at last, be restored

# Ripples 1

A bomb explodes, a tsunami strikes
A plane crashes, a government falls
And the world is changed forever
Those near and far
Impacted by events
Of such great enormity
Are despairing and dejected
Their lives will never be the same again
And hope is nowhere to be found
In the rubble and ruin created
The devastation caused
By these occurrences
Is easily seen
Their ripples knocking us for six
Their tide burying and drowning
The forlorn in its destructive wake
But there is chaos too
In the small things
The things of a seemingly
Inconsequential nature
A wing flaps, a pebble drops
A light goes out, a tap drips
Tiny things
Creating ripples
With vastly different outcomes
Altering the future
In ways we didn't expect
Butterflies with enormous power
To change the world forever

# Ripples 2

We are not nearly as insignificant as we think
For all that we do
And all that we say
Has an effect
That can be far wider
Than the space that we merely occupy
An effect beyond
What we already see and know
We don't always understand
The unfolding tide of fate
The consequences
Of what we have set in motion
We don't always realise
The possible repercussions
Of our words and deeds
We are far more significant than we think
Even the dark corners
Cannot cancel out or conceal
The ripples we create
Cannot hide the hurt or harm
That we may have birthed
Perhaps unintentionally
That might echo
On into the future
To the detriment
Of others

# Ripples 3

All these things have shaped me
Made me who I am
The sins of my fathers
Rippling through the ages
From their past
Down to my present
Their deeds, their words
Holding me fast
Enchained
The wounds of my friend
Inflicted so often unintentionally, unknowingly
But still creating
Deeply embedded shards
Cutting me to the quick
The actions of my family
Those very ones
Who should have loved me most
Nurturing, supporting
When all others failed to
Yet so often oblivious
Of what was needful
These things have shaped me
Left me torn, bruised and battered
Still reeling
From shock after shock
Shockwaves constantly shaking me
To the foundations
Of my very existence

# Ripples 4

Night dark, everything eerily still
All created things had long been on hold
Awaiting this moment
The moment that it was at last finished
The battle won
The enemy vanquished
Death defeated
Dead men walking
The curtain torn
The way laid wide open
Into the holiest place

This was a moment
That has lasted forever
What was accomplished then
Can never be undone
The clock can never be
Turned back
The deed
Never erased
Rippling down through time
Its earth-shattering, spine-tingling impact
Lives with us still
And now His victory is
Our victory
His conquest of death
Our eternal life
The enemy, under His footstool
Held captive
No longer has
Dominion over us
And freedom is ours

# London is a state of mind

No brook with strugglers
No patience with stragglers
This city
This vast, frantic metropolis
Home of a thousand generations
Sucks you in
Subsumes you
Brainwashes you into believing
That this minuscule corner of the universe
Is the most significant
The centre of everything

London is a state of mind
Its beating heart
Pulsates with the glories of years long gone
Its buzz drowns out
The desire for anything else
As it slots you into its hive
Its frenzy casts a spell on you
Absorbing you into its mindset
The conformity of its nonconformity
Its lie that anything goes
When in reality
Only that which fits the mould
Is the acceptable face of its reason

London is a state of mind
Its waterways and green pastures belie
calmness
For there is no peace here
But the constant race to succeed
To rush to a destination
That is always in the distance
That is always just out of reach

# The secret of the clay

From hard dry ground the clay was raised
Lifted high from stone-cold earth
And moulded, shaped with tender care
In hope of fellowship

With love, the breath of life was breathed
And clay became a living soul
Mere dust no more, the pinnacle
Of all created things

In faith was made a friend for Him
Who is the start and end of all
So full of life, this clay so rare
A secret treasure known

What wonderous thing, this living clay
Its heart attuned with Him who breathed
Into its heart, that man might be
In image of his Lord

And does the ground remember this
And think, in quiet moments, still
Of when the King of Earth and Heaven
Chose clay to fashion man

And does it cry in deep despair
That man, once drawn from its own stock
Now lives such deep disregard
Of that from whence he came

# One day

One day, the world will be redeemed
This sorry world
So damaged, broken, fragmented
Sliding down a slippery slope
Of collapse and cataclysm
One day, everything will be restored
The Lord, the Lord of the heavens and the Earth
Will make known His salvation
And all the ends of the Earth will see it
One day, green pastures and rugged mountains
Clear, still waters
And the multitude of living creatures
Will rejoice at the return of their King
One day, the Earth will again be glad
The hills will sing together for joy
The rivers will clap their hands
And trees will grow leaves
That bring healing to those
Who had once caused such harm
One day, lions and lambs will rest quietly
together
There will be no need for tears
And those who once made weapons of warfare
Will turn them into gardening tools
And live together in peace
One day, the world will be redeemed
But now, right now, it is groaning
Waiting, hoping for a soon advent of its
redeemer
Whilst those whom He had long ago
Appointed as its guardians
Continue to act with thoughtless disregard
For His directions

# Songs of the Children

A collection of poems about who we are, and the situations we find ourselves in

# I'm only human

I'm only human
Not perfect
Full of good intentions
But apt to fail, to fall short
Sometimes spectacularly
I'm prone to notice
All the tiny failings of others
Yet not be aware
Of the logs in my own eyes
Likely to angrily accuse others
Of their small indiscretions
But to always overlook
My own dramatic failures
Brushing them under the carpet
Where they cannot be seen
I'm only human after all

I'm only human
Not perfect
Always keen to appear
In a positive light
My faults and weaknesses
Disguised, camouflaged
That even those who know me
Do not come to realise
Who I truly am
Or think to draw back the curtain
Where they would find
What has been
Well-hidden for so long
Am I living a lie
Or is this normal life
I'm only human after all

# A song for the broken

Hold my heart, but gently
For it is fragile, hurting
This heart has been broken
Too many times now
And wounded beyond an easy mending

Hold my heart, but softly
For it is fearful, troubled
This heart has been damaged
Over and over
And bruised beyond a rapid healing

Hold my heart, but kindly
For it requires patience, gentleness
This heart needs steadfastness
A courage that will not
Easily give up or ever let go

Hold my heart, but lovingly
Keep anger, harshness far from its door
Tread softly, with hope
Believe in endless possibilities
That everything can indeed be renewed

Hold my heart, but expectantly
Knowing it is not forever lost
Its time to advance will soon come
And it will surely recover, be restored
Hold my heart, but in faith

# Tell me who I am

I seem to have lost my way
Through the maze of my existence
I peer into the depths of my being
Unsure of what I now see
My focus blurred
My purpose indistinct
My person obscured
Hidden in the labyrinth of my mind palace
I cannot seem to find myself
Or the sense of who I am
Have I changed beyond all recognition
My identity snatched away
And taken captive
Entangled in the unfathomable recesses
Of life's morass
Am I hiding even from myself
Tell me who I am
That I might know once more
All that You see
That I might find
All that I am
In You
That I might know myself
As I am known
Tell me who I am

# Hall of mirrors

I refuse to be defined by distorted mirrors
To allow myself
To be reflected in tainted glass
I long to see
A pure reflection
Of the person that I am
And am called to be
But in life's hall of mirrors
The images that I see
Are not the truth
Of my existence
For there, fragmented elements
From those around me
From past and present turmoil
Trap me between realities
Resulting in skewed perceptions
Of who I am
And cause me to believe the mirror's lie
That I am merely a grasshopper
When, in reality, I am a giant
That I am weak
When, in fact, I am strong
And fearful, when I have everything I need
To fight whatever is thrown at me
That rises up against me
For He that is in me
Is greater than the one
That opposes me
And when I see my reflection in His mirror
His pure, undistorted, unadulterated mirror
I see the truth of who
I am actually really meant to be

# A bewilderment of mirrors

Wherever we look
They are staring back at us
In this bewilderment of mirrors
A myriad of faces
Are reflected over and over
And we can see them
Far into the distance
In a confusion of repetition

From this wilderness of mirrors
Voices are calling to us
Their words
A cacophony of sounds
Raucous and strident
Incessant, insistent voices
Clamouring for our attention
Desiring our devotion
Assertive, angry voices
Aiming to strike fear into our hearts
Should we not succumb
To their entreaties to grasp hold of
Their illusions of happiness
And to conform to their ideals
But would rather dare to shatter
This disorientation of mirrors
Abandoning their shards
To lie silent on the cold hard ground

# Shards

Shards of my former existence
Still cause me pain
Their lingering fragments
Embedded in my heart
Are so difficult to root out
Pale shadows of my former self
Lurk out of sight
But never quite out of mind
Calling me, enticing me
Back to where I started
Hidden from prying eyes
Their voice is crying out
Reaching deep into my mind
Over and over it whispers the lie
That what was before
Was so much better
Than what is now
Its pull is so strong at times
That it is difficult to resist
A super-human strength is needed
To draw these shards from my heart
Fearless of the consequences
Believing that this would bring healing not harm
And that they would disturb me no longer
Once removed
They must be placed far away
Where they cannot be seen or heard
So that their desires for me
And their affect upon me
Are finally of no consequence

# The unknown

A gigantic gawping cavern
Swallowing all that crosses its path
The unknown is the great fear bringer
A real life-changer
No solid foundation there
No clear way forward evident
Its unsettling presence
Overwhelms every waking thought
Makes restless every interminable night
And drowns every hope for the future
In the swell of its tears
Pervading all attempts
To bring clarity and direction
It is an invisible monster
We can never completely vanquish
Unable to grasp hold of
Its tangled tentacles
In order to unravel its threats and lies
The unknown sets our hearts racing
And causes our hand to tremble
Incapacitating us with anxiety
And immobilising us with fear
Such is the extent of its power
Its hold over us

# Rumours of war

We have always known that there would be
Wars and rumours of war
But, lulled into a false sense of security
We never expected that right here, right
now
In our day, in our time
Like a thief in the night
It would creep in amongst us
Catching us unawares
For we had foolishly thought
That the past was an adequate teacher
That such vile things as have happened
before
In our own sphere
Could not happen right here, again and now
But yet they are
People just like us
People not far away from us
Forced into subterranean lives
As their world above is demolished
Fleeing in tortoise-like convoys
To perceived places of security
In dread of the obliteration
Of their own land
Remembering another time
When it was so quickly snatched away from
them
Whilst those whose end goal is subjugation
Head relentlessly towards their powerless
prey

# Song of the fallen

And still they clamour for our attention
The fallen, flung in far-off fields and trenches
The lost, languishing in swamp-ridden jungles
The undeserving of untimely execution, deep in
murky forests
And of cruel extermination in vermin-infested camps
These fallen of the past
Who gave up freedom once, in freedom's hope
Or had it snatched away
Did they all die in vain

Their blood does cry out still
That we would fight for peace
That only love should conquer all
And love might win the day
But yet we heedless are
The fallen's cries unheeded yet
For hearts and minds in anger
Rouse passions better left
And so we yearn for war
And unremittingly fight
Over words and ideologies
Over lands and for commodities
Thus nations rise and fall
With little thought at times
Of those who dwell within
Who languish even yet
The fearful, broken, wounded
The fallen of our day
And they too cry how long
How much must be endured
Before our cries can cease
And we can dwell, at last
In peace

# Spitfire

Free as a bird
For freedom's sake
You flew
Soaring over England's
Green and pleasant land
So much owed to you
By so many
How could we ever repay such a debt
And still
We are free

With grace you glide yet
A gallantry unsurpassed
By any other
This sceptred isle is fortunate
That you remain above us
Dipping and diving
Over white cliffs and wide malls
The memory will not fade
For still
You roar freedom

# Blood on the ground

To the ground it fell
Over and over again
Its repetition unnoticed
The suffering of multiple generations
Their entreaties for justice
Unheeded
No catalyst for change evident
The blood on the ground
Mourns the hollow words
That never led to freedom
And yet this blood cries out still
Through years of silence
Calling to us
That we should shout
No more!
This blood is pleading with us now
Its lament rising
From every paving stone
Ascending to every rooftop
Hovering over streets and homes
This blood cries out
No more division of inequality
Or deception of hypocrisy
Clamouring for our attention
With no guarantee of change
The blood on the ground
Demands our action
Its hope
That some will
At last
Listen

# Living through history

The future is not yet known
But we are living through history in the making
We long to wipe the slate clean
Put it all behind us
As if it had never actually happened
But this annus horribilis
Will prove impossible to forget
And will one day be the stuff of history books
Children everywhere will learn
Of the time when the world stood still
Gawping at an encroaching and accelerating
horror
When life was left on hold
Held hostage at the whim of a rampant virus
Psychologists and historians not yet born
Will study, analyse and write their PhDs on
The resultant political pandemonium, economic
upheavals
Emotional turmoil and enforced imprisonments
Considering how and why all held dear
Indeed, even life itself
Was kept perpetually hanging by a thread
And how the world changed forever
For this has been a year like no other
One that we would never care to repeat
But one that has taught us to value
What is truly important
We hope against hope
That things will soon be different, better
Hardly daring to hope
That the end is actually in sight
That the promise of much longed-for freedom
Will actually materialise
But the future is not yet known

# Becoming

I have not yet become
But I am becoming
Not yet fully formed
But a work in progress
Not falling apart
But falling into place
Not breaking down
But breaking through
Into the light
The light of a new day
I have not yet arrived
But I am on my way

The end is not in sight yet
It's a long way ahead
But I have my eyes
On the final destination
My mind is fixed
On the ultimate goal
One step at a time
And I will get there
I am not finished
But I know where I'm heading
I have not yet become
But I am becoming

# Keep the end in sight

Keep the end in sight
The ultimate goal
For all that is waiting for you
At the end of this race
Will be worth the extreme effort
The pain and the hardship
That you will have to go through
To get there
Keep the end in sight
Do not give up at the first hurdle
Or cave in at the first sign of trouble
This race is not one for the faint-hearted
There will be many obstacles to overcome
And problems to surmount
Along the way
Keep the end in sight
The road is long and winding
And you will not reach your destination quickly
For this race, this journey
Takes a lifetime
But know, please know
That you are not going it alone
For if you listen, listen hard
You will hear a great crowd
Cheering you along
These are the ones
Who have run this race before you
Who have already won their prize
And they know
Yes they know
That it was all worth it

# It is high time

It is high time that you stepped
Into all that I have planned for you
From the beginning
I have waited patiently for you
For so long
Seemingly endlessly
For you to come into the realisation
That my desires for you
Are for your good
And my heart for you
Overflows with love and acceptance
And for you to want to let me in
It is time that you opened wide the door
To your heart
That I might enter fully
Into your life
But know this
When I am let in
I am not looking
To remain only in a small dark, dusty corner
But to hold your heart in my hands
To fuse it into my heart
To feel your every heartbeat
Share your every thought
That I might sit with you
And you with me
So that as we talk heart to heart
You would come to know me
As you are already known

# This love

If I descend to subterranean caverns
Or ascend to heavenly heights
If I journey to the far reaches of the Earth
Or search high and low my whole life long
I will never find
Never reach
The edge of this love
The place where this love ends
Its beating heart is never still
Its blazing fire never goes out
Its bottomless well never runs dry
Nothing can diminish or destroy it
Nothing can quench or quell it
Nothing can erase or extinguish it
This love never fails
Its heart never breaks
Never cracks
It is never too small to hold your heart
It sets you in its sights
Seeks you out
And never lets you go
This love only has the best intentions
The most incredible plans
And the clearest vision of far horizons
It constantly whispers your name
Calling you home
To stay close
Not stray far
This love never abandons hope
Never gives up
Always draws out the best
Always encourages more
And is always freely given
Surpassing any other

It is worthy of all you can give
All that you have
This love

# This anchor

This anchor holds me fast
Even in the wildest storm
When everything is raging all about me
This anchor will keep me securely fixed
To solid ground
When the wind howls wild
And the waters swell
This anchor remains firm
And I stay safe
When the thunder roars
And the lightning cracks
I do not need to be afraid
For I am preserved
Out of harm's way
And there is nothing, nothing
That can separate me
From His love
No raging or evil thing
No threatening circumstance
No terror, real or imagined
For all these must submit
To the One who loves me
And who holds me fast
With His anchor

# Shalom

This peace that He has given us
Is totally outside our comprehension
Completely beyond our normal worldly
experience
More than we could ask or dream of
This peace is a fulness of flourishing
A totality of tranquillity
A completeness of concord
Bringing wholeness and well-being
It encompasses us
Leaving us refreshed, renewed
This peace is our destiny and our aim
For in it we are blessed
And bringing it we are known
To be His children
In this peace we are overcomers
No longer afraid, we can dwell secure
This peace stills the racing heart
Assuages the adversaries
Reconciles the divided
And restores hope in desperate times
In this peace that He has given us
We are truly blessed
For everything good that we desire
And all that we could ever need
Is there

# Benediction

May His love enfold you
In the vast expanse of His embrace
May His strength sustain you
That you might not slip or fall
May His power protect you
And preserve you from every evil
May His grace flow freely
Flooding your life with His lovingkindness

For yours is the favour of the Lord
You are established in righteousness
Blessed with peace
And set apart for fruitfulness

May you always know the warmth of His
approval
And the radiance of His shining presence
Illuminating your way
May you hear Him singing over you
Rejoicing that He has captivated your heart
May you enjoy His bountiful goodness
Pouring over you
Filling all your empty places
And washing away every remembrance
Of past hurt and harm

# There's a song in all of us

Can you hear the song inside you
Have you chosen yet to let it out
For a song will make the fragile heart strong
A song can set the imprisoned spirit free
A song causes the weary soul
To rejoice and be glad
So look hard inside of you
Search high and low
The whole depth and breadth
Of your inner being
Your song will be there
For there is a song in all of us
Just listen
Though it may lie deep down, deep within
And, as yet, perhaps may only be as a broken
fragment
You can find it and you will recognise it
For it is your song
And when you do find it
Lay hold of it and set it free to soar
Wherever you are, sing
However you feel, sing
Whatever you do, sing
Sing alone, sing with others
Sing gently in the quiet and stillness
Sing loudly from the mountain tops
Let your song nourish you and bring you peace
Let your song renew you and bring you joy
Wherever you are
However you feel
Whatever you do
Sing!

# Songs for the Shepherd

A collection of poems
based on Psalm 23

# Psalm 23

The LORD is my shepherd, I lack nothing.
He makes me lie down in green pastures,
he leads me beside quiet waters,
he refreshes my soul.
He guides me along the right paths
for his name's sake.
Even though I walk
through the darkest valley,
I will fear no evil,
for you are with me;
your rod and your staff,
they comfort me.
You prepare a table before me
in the presence of my enemies.
You anoint my head with oil;
my cup overflows.
Surely your goodness and love will follow me
all the days of my life,
and I will dwell in the house of the LORD
forever.

# This shepherd

The One who
Is my shepherd
Will never leave me or forsake me
For I am always on His mind
His heart is always for me
And all His plans for me are good
With the One who is my shepherd
I will never get lost
Because He leads me in the way
Taking me along straightforward paths
To quiet waters and
Lush green meadows
And follows me behind
Ensuring that I do not
Give up or give in
When I stumble or falter
Or grow tired and weary
He breathes His life into me
Refreshing my body
And restoring my soul
I have complete confidence in Him
For He never fails
His well never runs dry
And His goodness and love
Are with me and upon me
Always

# You give me all I need

All the abundant riches
Of Heaven are Yours
The enormity of eternity
The vastness of an infinitude of universes
Belong to You
Yet You
The King of all kings
The Lord of all things
Abandoned these magnificent splendours
And chose to enter our small world with
nothing
Pouring Yourself out
Into humanity
For us
For me
Giving Yourself away
To us
To me
And in You to whom belongs all things
Can be found
All that is needed for
Life eternal
Life in all its fulness
And so, I will never be in want
For You give me all I need

# He makes me lie down

The pace of life these days
Is unrelenting
There is no time to stop and stare
To stand and gaze
To breathe deeply, slowly
To reflect, to simply be still
And to be fully present in each amazing
moment
And so
Creation's magnificence and grandeur
And life's incredible marvels
So often simply pass us by
And so too
We are worn down
With the incessant urge
To hurry, hurry, hurry
And fill every waking moment to the brim
With all that demands to be done
But He who holds all things together
He who neither slumbers nor sleeps
Calls us to come to Him
He makes us lie down and rest
So that He can refresh, re-energise and renew
us
And restore our souls
He calls us to be still
And simply to be
With Him

# But where are the green pastures?

But where are the green pastures
For all I can see before me
Is a desolate rocky wasteland
And rugged distant mountains
The haunt of wild things

I long for green pastures
The promised tranquil oasis
With glass-clear, glass-still waters
And long, cool, fresh grass
Oh to sit and gaze out
On such a beautiful vista
To know the peace of greenness
The restoration of my soul

Oh where are the green pastures
Deep to deep I hear them calling
Drawing me to that forever garden
The place of my heart's yearning
My forever home

# Quiet waters

Like a mirror
It reflects clouds
Scurrying across the heavens
Such extreme blueness
Punctured by a stream
Of wispy cotton
And the occasional avionic trail
Edged by luscious greenness
This place is hauntingly peaceful
Here, it is easy to centre my heart
On Your goodness and mercy
And to quieten my mind
From its incessant rushing
To be released from agonising over
Life's punishing cruelties
These quiet waters
Create in me the elusive stillness
That I always long for
The safe-haven
That I so dearly need
This is a place
Where I can find myself
And unearth the treasure
That is in my heart

# You restore my soul

When I am weak, worn out and exhausted
You restore my soul
When I am burnt-out, battle-fatigued and war-
weary
You restore my soul
When I am lost, lonely and dismayed
You restore my soul
When I am alone, abandoned and rejected
You restore my soul
Your water is alive
It cleanses and refreshes me
Splashing over barren places
Releasing hope
Your light vanquishes darkness
Subduing fear
Extinguishing despair
Your blood overcame the evil one
Defeating death
Unleashing freedom
You draw me to Your side
Hold me close
Whisper the truth
That I am loved
That I am valued
That I am Yours
And You restore my soul

# He will guide you

Life can be confusing
Uncertain
Troubling
The way ahead is not always evident
Or straight forward
It can be shrouded in mist
With zero visibility
Obscure
Impossible to know which path to take
Or which door to open
The mind perplexed and befuddled
By an endless swirling of possibilities
An overabundance of options
Or sometimes
Of no evident viable option at all
So, the heart can be unsettled
Perturbed
Downcast
With fear arising and paralysing
But stop
Do not forget that He is there
He is with you
He is always with you
Walking before you and beside you
He will be your guide
He will illuminate your path
And direct you to the good way
Be still and listen to His still small voice
Which is calling to you
Through every storm
Peace be still
Follow me

# The valley of shadows

This place is not my home
This haunt of shadows
This place of despair
This darkness is not my habitation
This murky gloom of hopelessness
Not my permanent abode
I will not remain
In the place
Where wicked things disturb
For though I may walk
Through dark valleys
Beside me, the One
Who shelters me
Is always the Rock
That will not fail
My dwelling place is His house
Where all is still
Where all is peace
Where goodness and mercy
Always surround those
Who trust in Him

# It is time to get out of the valley

I have been too long in this dreary valley
This place of shadows
Where evil things lurk
A place of demoralising darkness
Where a suffocating heaviness
Pervades everything for as far as the eye can see
Bringing with it an apprehensiveness
A sense of hopelessness
And a feeling of despair
That crush the spirit
And contuse the soul
I am desperate to get out of this deathly valley
Yet I know that I need not be fearful
For even as I walk through this
Place of desolation
You are always there
Right there, beside me
And Your brightness irradiates the darkness all
around
Lifting its oppression
And cheering my dispirited heart
And I know too that in You I will lack no good
thing
For You will strengthen me
And not leave me lost in this tenebrous terrain
But You will lead me
To a place where the air is crisp and clean
To where there is sparkling clear water
And expansive green meadows
A place in which Your goodness and mercy
Are plain to see
And there is peace

# We will fear no evil

This world's darkness
Weighs down on us
Would oppress us
Overwhelm us
This world's darkness
Does attack us
Snatches from us
Peace and hope

But we will fear
We will fear no evil
Though we can hear
The lion snarling
And even if it comes so close
That we can see
The whites of its eyes
We know that we will be safe
In You

And we will trust
We will trust in You Lord
Though nations
Rise and fall
And enemies who wish us harm
Surround us
On every side
We know that we will be safe
With You

# Walk in His peace

Walk in His peace
For in that peace
The disquiet of your soul will be stilled
And you will feel life's turbulence
Can no longer knock you off balance
In that peace
Your heart will know liberation
From the fears that constantly overwhelm you
And you will know that all things can be well
And work together for your very good
His super-human peace
Is quite beyond the confines of our human
comprehension
Something that we cannot fully get our heads
around
For we consistently fail to dwell in peace
To be at peace
To walk in peace
Our lives beset by multitudinous things
So much unresolved anger
So many still-festering wounds
But He who is Himself peace itself
Can be your peace
He who stilled raging storms
Is walking across the frenzied waters towards
you
Saying peace, be still
Lift up your head, look now
He is fast approaching
Walking towards you
That you might walk in peace
With Him

# A table stands before me

A table stands before me
Beside the tranquil waters
And there
A feast to refresh my soul
Has been prepared
By One who delights in me
By One who knows
Exactly what I need
And all that I desire
And so
I lack nothing
And my heart overflows with joy
My enemies stand around me watching
Calling out to me
Hoping to gain entrance
To my feast
And a foothold in my heart
But I am not afraid
And will not invite them to come
And sit down at my table
For this table is for me
And me alone

# That other feast

There is another feast
Spread before us on a table
Enticing things, piled high
Drawing us over to gaze upon them
Calling to us
To taste and eat them
This feast looks too good to be true
For everything we have ever dreamed of
Everything that we could possibly desire
Is there
And so it is
But as you come closer
As you look carefully
You will realise that this feast
Is a feast of no good thing
But a feast of lies and deception
A feast of anger and fear
A feast of pain and heartache
If you are ambushed by its attractiveness
And fooled by its magnetic mendacity
This feast will entrap you
So wake up, wake up quickly
Before you are held captive
By its delights
Do not be lured by its fleeting vanities
Do not sit down at this table
For if you do
You will be held hostage
By one who means you only harm

# Squeezed

Sometimes, it feels like
I am being squeezed and squeezed
Into a smaller and smaller space
That, crushed and hemmed in on every side
I am gradually being reduced
To almost nothing
I know that the enemy of my soul
Desires to eliminate me
To overwhelm me
With feelings of insignificance and inadequacy
To prevent me from rising up
And seizing hold of
God's goodness and mercy
And all that
He has planned and purposed
For me
But then I stop and remember
Who I really am
For to Him who loved me from the beginning
I am not a nothing or a nobody
But His beloved one
His chosen possession
The apple of His eye
And He is calling me to come
And be with Him
And to know
That His goodness and mercy
Will follow me always

# You anoint our heads with oil

Yours is the oil of gladness
And this oil
That You pour over us
Is to bless us
And to fill us
With every good thing

Yours is the oil of holiness
And this oil
That You pour over us
Is to set us apart for You
To sanctify us
And consecrate us

Yours is the oil of healing
And this oil
That You pour over us
Is to restore us
To renew us
And to set us free

And Your cup
Is full to the brim
And the oil runs over
For You are a generous
Gift-giver

# I know and I am sure

I know and I am sure
That His goodness and mercy
Will always be with me
As He Himself is always with me

I know and I am sure
That nothing can snatch me away from Him
Or prevent me
From drawing close to Him

I know and I am sure
That I can be with Him where He is
And that I can live
In His presence forever

And there, I will fear no evil
And there, I will feast on the amazing things
That He has prepared for me
And there, to make my heart glad
He will pour His oil all over me
And I will be surrounded by His goodness and
love
Forever

# I would dwell in Your house

Some have said
That they would rather be doorkeepers
At Your house
But not me
I do not want
To merely stand outside on the threshold
Looking in
Where I can just catch glimpses
Of Your dwelling place
And be simply an observer
I long to come right inside
To be where You are
Oh, that I might stay with You
And You with me

I long to enter the heavenly realms
To peek into the holy place
Where You reside
To gaze upon Your majesty
And to behold Your glory
To listen to the song of Heaven
To hear Your voice
And to feel Your very heartbeat
For then I might truly know You
As I am known
Oh, that I might dwell Your house
Forevermore

# A song for the thirsty

I am the well
That no man has dug
The water that springs up from within
Is refreshing for your soul

I am the rain
That falls gently on arid ground
Washing away dust and ashes
Triggering abundant new green shoots

I am the springs
That break forth in the wilderness
Bringing cool streams and rivulets
That gush across parched desert lands

I am the fountain
That bubbles up with crystal clear water
All who go there to drink
Will never be thirsty again

I am the life-giving water
That can quench every thirst
And if you drink of me
You will live with me forever

I am the song
That is rejoicing over you
My water is alive
So if you are thirsty, come to me and drink

# Ode to the shepherd

Fresh and clean You fall
Like dew in the morning
You wash my cares away
You cleanse my soul
Clear and strong You rise
Like sunshine's bright dawning
You put the dark to flight
Make all things new

You are my brightest day
My song never-ending
You are my boundless joy
My richest prize
You are my soaring hope
And all my heart's yearning
You are my ocean wide
My deepest calm

Firm and sure You stay
Like towering mountains
You do not shrink or change
You're always there
And through the night You shine
Like dazzling starlight
Upon my darkest way
Exploding joy

# Songs to the Father

## A collection of poems based on The Lord's Prayer

# The Lord's Prayer
## Matthew 6:9-13

This, then, is how you should pray: Our Father in heaven, hallowed be your name, your kingdom come, your will be done, on earth as it is in heaven. Give us today our daily bread.

And forgive us our debts, as we also have forgiven our debtors. And lead us not into temptation, but deliver us from the evil one.

For yours is the kingdom and the power and the glory forever and ever. Amen.

# Our Father

Not like any earthly, human father
You are
For Your love for us
Is vaster, broader
More constant, consistent

Bottomless, fathomless
It is unlike any other love
That we have ever known
Or experienced
Can ever know
Or experience

Not dependent on our love for You
On our desire to love You in return
Your love
Requires no recompense
Seeks no reward
But reaches out to us
In spite of all we may have done
Or are
Giving us all we need
Working all things together for our good

You are a father like no other
A father to the fatherless
A recoverer of the lost
A reviver of the wounded soul
A restorer of the orphan-hearted
You are always enough
Will always be enough
Our Father

# Heaven

The veil is so thin
A gossamer-like cobweb
Ethereal, diaphanous, almost see-through
That separates us from Heaven
The place where You dwell
And from You
For we inhabit a thin place
Where You are always near
Always with us
Emmanuel
But yet
We still imagine that veil of separation
To be as heavy velvet
Its hem weighted down
Impenetrable
Impossible to raise, to get through
That You are distant, out of reach
From us
That Your heavenly home
Is so remote
So beyond all that we can ever imagine
Even dream of
But yet
The curtain was long since
Torn in two
That we might step through
That we might find You
Encounter You
In the place where You dwell
That Heaven
Your home
Might also become
Our dwelling place

# Theophany

Why did God break out
Of that iridescent place
Which none might yet approach
Lest its scorching incandescence
Should melt away all
In the dark and dismal world
Of those who had forsaken Him
At the beginning
And of those who down and down
Through countless ages
Preferred Him not
Why did He constrict His eternal magnitude
Into such an insignificant smallness
Such a dingy drabness
As was the inception of His manifestation
To the world of men

Yet such eminence, restricted to commonness
Was triumph through innocence
The palpable demonstration of the abiding love
Of the infinite for the finite
The creator for the created
For this was the presentation
Of Emmanuel

# Holy

That far pavilion
His dwelling place
The place where He abides
Is far, far removed from us
And so beyond our wildest imaginings
Our most superlative dreamings
The splendour and magnificence
Of that holy place
Can never be truly, fully visualised
By our limited human minds
Or ever adequately described
By our mere human words

From beyond the far distant horizon
Beyond the highest heavens
The throne surrounded by radiant heavenly
beings
The holy place
His eternal home
The sound of many waters rises up
A never-ending song
Of unceasing praise
A perpetual standing-ovation
To the everlasting One
For there and from there
The King unlike any other
Reigns forever and ever
For all glory and majesty
Wisdom, power and authority
Belong to Him, the Holy One

# Is it a pointless exercise?

Is it a pointless exercise
To try to put into words
Something beyond words
To describe
Something indescribable
Is there any value at all
In attempting to imagine
Something so far removed
Far distant
From my wildest, craziest imaginings
If I sit right still, close my eyes
And think hard, dream hard
Will what my feeble human mind can conceive
Ever bear even the slightest relation
To the heavenly reality
Can I ever get anywhere near
To that holy, heavenly place
Where He dwells
Near enough perhaps to at least be a doorkeeper
Able to stand just outside
And try to obtain a glimpse of what's within
Is it a pointless exercise
A hopeless ambition

But what I do know
Is that the King of the Ages
The King of the heavens and the Earth
Has reached down
To find me where I am
Leaving His heavenly abode
To become
Emanuel

# Those who would fly

God is seeking eagle men
Those who would fly to the highest heights
To be with Him, where He is
Who would dare to reach His dwelling place
And rest with Him there in that heavenly abode
Those who would rise on the thermals
Soaring, climbing tirelessly higher and higher
Until the wind of His Spirit
Carries them so close
That they can hear
Even the gentlest whisperings of His voice
And resonate the very beatings
Of His heart
God is seeking eagle men
Those who can see afar from the heights
And grasp that which is beyond mere knowledge
Understanding the things that are and are not
But those who would fly so
Must set all else but Him aside
And be still
As they await the unforced gift
Of His unwearying strength
That is the source of eagle soaring

# The name

So much meaning in this name
This name like no other
Higher than any other
Greater than all others
Indescribably magnificent, ineffably vast
In scope, in time
How can we even attempt to elucidate
Quantify or pin down
What is beyond understanding
Or to put into words
What cannot be held, or truly grasped
For in this name is a power inconceivable
To mere mortals
In this name are a splendour and holiness
Found nowhere else
Yet, in this name we see and can know
A love without borders
A peace beyond understanding
A goodness never ceasing
Righteousness and justice
Salvation and freedom
For all
Undeserving as we are
And we all, irrespective of person, may approach
And enter that Holy Place
Where He, the Holy One, dwells
For He, the author and finisher
The one who is the beginning and the end of all
things
Has made a way for us
He is our father
And His desire
Is to make His dwelling place with men

# This kingdom

The shining bounds of this kingdom
Are not always evident
Or visible to the naked eye
But they are available to be discerned
By those who can see beyond seeing
And hear beyond hearing
For this kingdom
Is unlike any other we know
Or have read about
In this world's realm
It is not defined by power struggles and internal
strife
By warring factions and dissatisfied citizens
The evidence of earthly kingdoms
But by the incredible majesty
Inconceivable beauty
And magnificent vision
Of its King
Its ways of gentleness
And paths of peace
Its fortresses of faithfulness and sacrifice
Are defined by His Words, His example
This kingdom knows no end
Its sphere is limitless
Its timespan is everlasting
Yet any who so desires and simply asks
Can enter
And dwell within it

# If Your will was done

If Your will was done in the Earth
Then all would choose You, love You, worship
You
Fall down before You
And lift You higher than all
If Your will was done in the Earth
Your created ones would
Cherish all You have made
Nurture every living thing
Carefully tend the lands they inhabit
If Your will was done in the Earth
There would be no war, no wounding
No violence, no wanton destruction
And all would lie down in safety, rest securely
And dwell in peace
If Your will was done in the Earth
We would walk in righteousness before You
And deal justly with others
Without lies and deceit
As all would dwell harmoniously together
If Your will was done in the Earth
The desires of Your heart
Would be our greatest desires
The plans You purpose
Would be the plans we pursue
And we would see things
How You see them
For we would look at everything
Through Your eyes

# He gives us all we need

The insatiate desire for more and more
To be the focus of a thousand eyes
Is the interminable yearning
Of so many hollow hearts
The vacuous dream
Of so many senseless souls
Building up treasure in barns
The preoccupation of those
Who cannot see beyond the here and now
Who do not realise that all this
Lasts but fleetingly
And is not all there is
Is not the main event
That all that we need
Is not in a moment's
Captivating craving
But in the One who
Gives us all we need
Is all we need
For He
Who is the beginning and end of all things
The One who holds all things together
Is the source and the foundation
Of everything that really matters
And when we
Thirst for Him
Drink deep of Him
He gives us all we need
Life in all its fulness
Life forevermore
Life in Him

# Sin

Sin separates
Sin divides
Sin imprisons
Man from God
Man from man
Man from the Earth
A poison leaving wreckage in its wake
Ravaging relationships
Annihilating accord
Triggering tumult
Its tendrils entwine, enmesh
Until there is no escape
From their constraining clutches
Sin was a thief from the beginning
A destroyer of all that is good
From a beautiful garden, ravaged by thistles
To a world torn asunder by war
Death became the destination of everything
When the ones who had once
Walked together in the cool of the day
Chose to turn their backs
On a loving Father
In order to gain the knowledge
Which would ultimately sow the seeds
Of the destruction of all that
He had created for them

# Forgive us

Love keeps no record of wrongs
No list to constantly mull over
To keep their memory alive
But flings them
Further than the eye can see
Buries them deep down
Deeper even than the deepest ocean ridge
So that they are gone forever
Love gave up everything
Even life itself
To forgive us
That we might walk free
No longer ensnared in the bondage
Of dark deeds
The desperate actions
Of an aphotic mind
Or the shortcomings
Of a feeble heart
Love refuses to remember
The tally totally wiped out
Its dispensation of absolution
Freely given
Should be freely received
No temporary reprieve here
But an acquittal of always
For love keeps no record of wrongs
Forgiveness is its beating heart
Its very lifeblood
And it asks only that
As you have freely received
You freely give

# As we forgive those

It is so hard for us to let go of
All the wrongs done to us
All the hurts inflicted upon us
All those who have wished us ill
Never mind seventy times seven
We can barely manage seven
To put such things behind us
And to move forward
Not letting the past
Define our future
Is challenging
Easier said than done
Forgiveness is sometimes
A gargantuan task
Not something we can easily conjure up
By mere willpower and determination
So much has built up over time
An edifice that is nigh impossible to scale
Or to demolish
Words and deeds that keep resonating
Hold us fast
Imprison us
Destroy us
But yet a choice is needed
If we are to live in freedom
And to grasp hold
Of all that is there for us
A choice
That does not deny the past
But that does prevent it
From robbing us of
Our future

# Those who sin against us

Those who have sinned against us
Can only continue to do us harm
If we allow them to
If we will not
Cannot
Let go
And walk away
From their evil words or deeds
But relive, reimagine them
Over and over
It is imperative for our emancipation
That we place them far, far behind us
And consciously abandon them there
That we might breakthrough
Into freedom
But, if we do not
Those who have sinned against us
Will keep us, sometimes unwittingly
In perpetual bondage
Held fast to the past
Trapped in what has gone before
Unable to walk into
The joys and delights
Of the future

# Deliver us from all evil

We know that the Prince of this World
Has planned our downfall
From the beginning
His heart of wickedness
Longs to ruin every created thing
For his desire
Is to destroy every beautiful thing
To rob us
Of every good thing
To separate us
From the fountain of life
From Him who has chosen us
And loved us
From the beginning
To steal our joy and peace
And to cause us
To spiral downwards
Into the darkness
And so
There is war
War in the heavenly places
War on the Earth
War all around us
War within us
Yet we know too
That He who rides
On the wings of the wind
Is He that is in us
And He will deliver us from all evil
So, we are more than conquerors
And nothing, nothing
Can separate us
From Him

# Walking out of the darkness

Cleanse us oh Lord
May Your searing light
Brighter than a thousand, thousand fires
Blaze up
And burn away our sin
Cauterising our hearts
That we might be fit
To abide in Your presence
Erase the wickedness of our past generations
That we and our children's children
Might dwell forever in abundant freedom
Flow down to us like water
And drown our sorrows in Your eternal deeps
Assuage the fears that immobilise us
And cast a shadow across our way
Wipe away our anguish and heartache
Heal our being
And transform our seeing
Nourish our souls
And set our spirits free
To run on the mountains
And soar above the heights
As we walk out of the darkness
And run exultant
Into Your splendorous light

# Power and glory

An insatiable desire to display power
To ensure that all are well aware
Of their ultimate authority
Results in regular demonstrations of
Pomp and circumstance
Military might
Monumental ostentatious palaces
And the manifest accumulation of vast wealth
Such are the evidences of earthly rulers
Yet You
Whose glory outshines the sun
Outshine it all
For Yours
Are the innumerable celestial arrays
The brightness of a thousand thousand stars
The imperium of the vast heavenly armies
For You
The nations of the Earth
Are as drops in a bucket
Their rulers, as mere grasshoppers
Their citizens as grains of sand upon a shore
But You
Are preeminent, illimitable
Lord over all things
Your dominion knows no bounds
Your power will never diminish
And Your glory will never cease

# Forever

We, who are so small
So very finite
So utterly limited by time and place
Cannot even begin to envisage
Eternity
Its immensity, its infinitude, its
immeasurability
Its far, far beyondness
However hard we try
Not even the most advanced telescopes
The most eminent physicists
Or the most learned philosophers
Can get anywhere near to doing so
But You
You are Alpha and Omega
The Beginning and the End
The Eternal One
Who was and is, and always shall be
You put everything that is into place
You set everything that is in motion
And You will begin the end of time
For You are forever
And You, the Eternal One
Have put eternity in our hearts
That burning desire, that restless yearning
Deep, deep within our souls
For forever
For more than meets the eye
For far distant horizons
For worlds beyond worlds
And for connection with the One
Who is forever

# About the author

Barbara lived, worked and worshipped in east London for over 35 years, where she was a teacher, headteacher and then a Senior Lecturer in Education at the University of East London. She was on the leadership team of her local church, for which she was also the worship co-ordinator, before retiring and moving, more recently, to south west London. In addition to writing poetry, she has written many songs for use in church and school, including a musical for children, Mighty Moses, whose initial performances involved 250 children. Barbara enjoys all kinds of music, visiting art exhibitions and museums, painting, singing in a local community choir, reading historical whodunits and spending time with friends and family. Barbara's first collection of poems, 'The Stones are Still Singing', a poetic narrative for Christmas and Easter, was published in 2015 by Zaccmedia, and has been used in Christmas and Easter services, retreats, dance workshops and a range of church meetings and events. A subsequent volume, 'Songs for the Journey', a collection of poetry about the journey that is life, was published by Zaccmedia in 2019. During the first covid lockdown, in April 2020, Barbara joined an on-line poetry writing group, and most of the poems in this new volume were initially shared during its weekly zooms.

# Other books by Barbara Todd

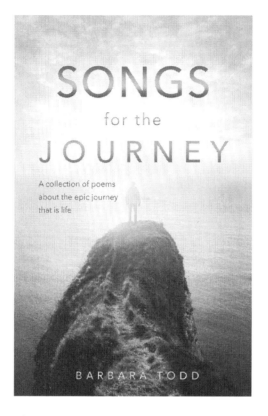

'Songs for the Journey' is a collection of poems that pose questions around where our true happiness should lie. The book gently takes us on a journey from some of the pressing personal issues of today, such as busyness, technological distractions, painful losses, hurt and depression, to a more joy-filled future. Developing a narrative of hope, the poems challenge us to reflect on our own lives and to place greater value and focus on things that last, and on where we are ultimately heading.

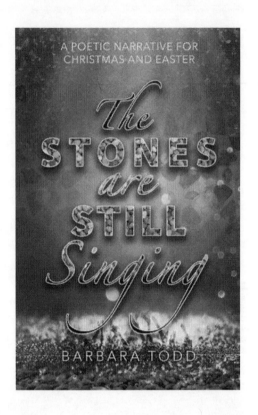

A POETIC NARRATIVE FOR
CHRISTMAS AND EASTER

The
STONES
are
STILL
Singing

BARBARA TODD

More than a collection of beautiful poems, this book resources schools and churches with a vivid narrative that runs across both Christmas and Easter. As a former primary school teacher and church worship co-ordinator, the author brilliantly retells the two most powerful stories of the Bible, making these poems ideal for special assemblies, Christmas plays and carol and Easter services. The book is neither over simplistic for adults nor too difficult for children, but will add fresh inspiration into any public or private reading. The poems express the clarity and depth these special seasons bring. In some, the author has written as though in character, bringing a new perspective and intimacy to these most famous of stories.